The Entrepreneurial Mindset

The 5 Entrepreneurial Mindsets

By: Shanie Salmon-Godfrey,
NCMA, M.A.A

Contents

Acknowledgement

Patience and understanding is what comes to mind when I think about my husband, Gavin R. Godfrey. I'm forever grateful for all the love and support that you have shown me throughout the years. I could not have done it without you. You did an amazing job holding down the family while this book was in production. Thank you for the great job you are doing with our amazing son, Giovanni G. Godfrey. I love you guys.

Dedication

This book is dedicated to all the diamond entrepreneurs that have constantly been supporting me through the years and to every diamond entrepreneur that keeps shining under pressure.

The best quality of a diamond is, the bigger it is, the further you must dig to get it. Therefore, the bigger the dream, the deeper you must dig within yourself to fulfill it. Keep building even if you don't have all the tools and resources. Even if you are the only one that believes in your vision, that's enough reason to keep building.

To the diamond entrepreneurs, dream bigger and reach higher.

Cheers to us!

"We don't quit, we elevate". - Shanie Salmon-Godfrey, NCMA, MAA

Introduction

The entrepreneurial mindset is written for entrepreneurs of all levels to transform the way that they think; elevate their businesses; and empower them to do it for someone else. Whether you are in the "idea" phase of your journey, in the process of starting a business, or growing your business, there are five stages that all entrepreneurs must go through in order to have a successful business. Regardless of your industry, the one thing that all entrepreneurs have in common is the five entrepreneurial mindsets.

This book is to help entrepreneurs identify the five entrepreneurial mindsets, with practical tools to overcome them. Throughout this book, we are going to explore different thought patterns, strategies, behavior patterns, and environmental influences that affect entrepreneurs along their journey. We will excavate those areas of our life, to start the entrepreneurial journey. With a written strategy, and proven steps to overcome them. For us to become entrepreneurs, we must launch that business. Let's dive in. The most important thing to consider before starting a business is identifying your reason for starting it. The reason for starting a business will keep your passion burning for your vision.

The entrepreneurial journey is one that's less traveled. It is a lonely journey that will often leave you feeling alone. The three things that you want to have in place before beginning your journey are:

1. Knowing Your Why.

Why am I starting a business? Everyone's why is unique to their life, calling, and purpose. Is it for you or your family? Is it to prove the world wrong? Most entrepreneurs start a business, not because they really want a business, but they want to prove somebody wrong. This is the worst reason to start a business. Starting a business is difficult and time-consuming. It requires a lot of money and sacrifices. If you are starting a business to make someone else happy, when things get difficult, the first thing you will want to do is to give up and go back to what is familiar and comfortable. No one wants to be uncomfortable. When we are placed in an uncomfortable situation, our brain is designed to do two things: fight or flight. We will fight through the difficulties or run back to our safe place.

2. Who Is in My Support System?

A support system is one of our greatest assets as an entrepreneur. This is often the stage that is often overlooked. Entrepreneurs often start their business with the mindset that they can do it alone. It's never as hard as it seems, until you launch that business. The truth is, your support system will be your most valuable asset. There will be situations that will make you want to give up and go back to comfort. However, your support system is to keep you from going back to comfort. The type of support system that you should have in place is not a support system that is going to be your cheerleader, stroke your ego, or make you feel good.

This support system is there to help you recognize where you are heading to, and to keep you on track with your vision. New entrepreneurs will often complain of lack of support simply because they expect people to commend them for everything they do. It is important to remember, they are there to push you, not to praise you. They are there to light a fire underneath you, to set you on fire for your business, and hold you accountable to yourself and your business. They will bring you back to your vision, when you are getting ready to quit.

3. What Is Stopping Me from Building My Business?

Entrepreneurs are told to plan for success. Not only do we need to plan for success, we also need to plan for failure. Whatever is stopping you from building your business today is going to be the same thing that's going to stop you from building your business later in your entrepreneurial journey. We must identify our risk factors and underwrite our risk. We must create a plan for success as well as our failures. Set realistic goals. Goals help with the navigation of fear. Fear is energy, if it is used correctly. Energy is defined as the strength needed to carry out physical and mental activities. Once we are afraid, we will activate fight or flight responses.

Every entrepreneur is fueled by fear of some sort. It could be as simple as fear of not being able to pay their bills, or fear of getting fired from a job. The most important thing to remember about fear is, it is not written in your DNA. You do not have the spirit of fear, but boldness, power, and a sound mind (2 Timothy 1:7). It takes equal amount of energy to fight as it does to flight. Use that energy to push yourself towards transformation. Energy cannot be destroyed, it can only be transferred. Transfer the way that you use fear. Use fear to underwrite your risk.

The first stage of entrepreneurship requires true transformation. True transformation begins with admitting that something needs to be change. You must make up in your mind to make the change. To change your mindset from where you are now to get to where you want to be. To find your purpose and fulfill your destiny. According to Merriam-Webster dictionary, to transform means to change in composition or structure. To convert, transformation means the process of transforming. Transformation doesn't happen by accident, you must be intentional about your actions, as well as the decisions that you make. Change comes through the removal or depositing of something. When something is changed, it is not the same in physical structure, appearance, or function.

Whether you are a blue collar, white collar, or free-spirited entrepreneur, in order to be successful in your field, it requires change. Entrepreneurs fail to realize that mindset is everything. Most entrepreneurs are running their business with an employee mindset, which gives them employee results. Not every boss is an entrepreneur. This is one of the biggest issues that I see when big companies fail. They have people in leadership that are not entrepreneurs. As an employee, we are told customers are always right, to the point where employees are being mistreated by their customers. As an entrepreneur, you have the authority to work with people that you enjoy working with. Employees make what their boss tells them that they are going to make. It doesn't matter how great your skills are, you start off with a limit on your earning abilities. Your earning potential is dictated by your boss.

That type of system limits the way that people think. Most people lack creativity and often settle into an endless cycle of more work, less pay. They master their job duties and descriptions, to stay in alignment with their employers' vision. They stifle their creativity. This behavior is often carried over into their business, which often holds entrepreneurs back from earning the amount of money that they are capable of earning. They are often shy or even afraid of asking their clients or customers for money. This behavior comes from fear of asking their boss for a raise on the job, because of the fear of being fired, for asking for that raise.

Employees are afraid to ask for raises because they don't want to seem unhappy, as well as the fear of rejection. Bosses often minimize the skills and value of their employees for fear of the employees knowing how much they are worth. People will quit a job once they believe that they are worth more. Employees will work all year for a 3-5 percent pay increase. Based on the position that they are in, when you do the calculations, it is equivalent to less than one dollar pay raise. Employees often seek their employers' validation for their work, and often settle for what they tell them that they are worth.

Entrepreneurs must overcome this mindset, or they will let the customers make their own price. They are seeking validation from their customers. These entrepreneurs will have a lot of different prices for the same services based on the client that they are working with. The clients that respect their work will pay them the asking price, and there will be those that want the service for next to nothing. Instead of turning those clients down, they cut their prices for them and make just enough to get by.

As an entrepreneur, you can make as much money as you want. You can increase your income as you develop and improve your skills.

The better you become, the more money you can make. However, as an employee, the better you become, the less money you make. Employees must seek promotions or change jobs based on their newly acquired skills. Most entrepreneurs are broke because they have employee work ethics and employee earning mindset. If they put in 40 hours of work, their paycheck is a set amount. Entrepreneurs often carry this behavior over into their businesses and become an employee in their business and not a business owner. They get enough clients to pay their bills and that's where the building stops. There is a distinct difference between the earning potential of an entrepreneur and an employee. You have the potential to make unlimited amount of money with the right systems in place. You control how much you make. Here is an example: If I take you to the bank, give you a large shopping cart, and tell you to take as long as you need to fill your cart up with cash, then when you are satisfied, come out of the vault with your cart and keep what is in the cart. You wouldn't rush and throw the money in the cart and run out the door, would you?

Most people would take their time to make a solid plan for stacking those bills. You would start measuring the cart to see the size and brainstorm how many bills you can stack, and how many ways you can stack them, to get the most out of your opportunity. Being an entrepreneur gives you the opportunity to change lives, not just your life. You are to help your customers, clients, or patients to add value to their lives. Plan on how you can add value. Like measuring the shopping cart, think about ways that you can consistently transform your services to the next level.

THE 5 ENTREPRENEURIAL MINDSETS

The five entrepreneurial mindsets are 5 unique mindsets all entrepreneurs go through at one point or another along their journey. I am here to help you recognize the mindsets and give you practical tools to adopt and overcome them.

1. **THE PERFECTIONIST MINDSET**

2. **THE SABOTAGING MINDSET**

3. **THE FEAR-OF-LETTING-GO MINDSET**

4. **THE BUSYBODY MINDSET**

5. **THE SERVANT MINDSET**

Chapter 1 - The Perfectionist Mindset

The perfectionist mindset is the first and most dangerous of all the entrepreneurial mindsets. The perfectionist mindset keeps you from launching or growing that business. Brand anatomy and physiology are the two driving forces of the perfectionist mindset. This is the first stage that we must overcome, for us to embark upon the entrepreneurial journey. During this stage, entrepreneurs often get caught up in the appearance of their brands. They spend a lot of time researching their competitors' brand appearances, which often leaves entrepreneurs comparing themselves to their competitors. They start to look at their brand through their competitor's eyes. How do they look beside their competitors? They are more concerned about how they look to their clients and competitors than the function of their brand with their clients.

This is the stage that business owners enjoy the most, and get caught up in branding as in, the physical appearance of the brand and not the function of the brand. When it comes to branding a business, regardless of the goods or services that are being offered, it can make or break your business. While branding is important, do not get caught up in the anatomy of the brand and neglect the physiology. The brand anatomy and physiology go hand in hand. You cannot have one without the other.

Branding Anatomy

The anatomy of the brand is the physical structure and appearance such as the logo, website, brochures, business cards, T-Shirts, uniforms, to name a few of the most common branding methods that new entrepreneurs often focus on. When it comes to branding, we need to look at everything that concerns our brands such as slogans; quotes; team members; print materials, which include business cards, brochures, websites, banners, etc.; media presence such as social media, podcast, guest appearance, and so on; competitive advantages; assets; liabilities; strengths; alliances; and weaknesses. Entrepreneurs tend to worry more about their physical appearance and neglect systems. They are looking at the brand colors, websites, flyers, social post images, quotes, email signature, domain names, etc.

The danger with this is, while those things are very important, we need to worry more about systems and structures; systems and structure is what is going to ultimately create your brand identity. How are you effectively communicating with your clients and team members? What systems do you have in place to help you measure your company's overall performance, growth, income, and service delivery? We must be intentional about the services that we deliver and the culture that we create. People buy into a company's culture, and that brings us to our brand physiology.

The perfectionist mindset will consume the entrepreneur's time and money. They will spend a lot of time trying to get everything perfect. Reinventing the wheel. They often struggle to launch their business because they are trying to get everything perfect before they launch the business. They often push back launching their business with the hopes that they will accumulate more capital to contribute to the anatomy of the business. This behavior can go on for months, years, and even a lifetime. To overcome this mindset, shift your focus from the brand anatomy to the brand physiology.

Branding Physiology

The physiology of the brand is the function of the brand. How the brand operates. The brand physiology can make or break the brand. The physiology speaks to the brand culture. How the brand function.

The entrepreneurial journey is the road less traveled. Being an entrepreneur means that you will often be on your journey alone. Being alone is not always a physical process; it can be emotional, spiritual, and psychological. You will have to become someone completely different from the person that you are today. If you are a shy, conservative person, you will have to transform to be someone that's assertive. If you don't like sales, marketing, and networking, you will have to develop interest in them.. The physiology of our brand should be built on systems and functions. Systems must be put in place, to deliver the things that we are promising our customers or clients.

The trap that a lot of entrepreneurs fall into is overpromising and underdelivering. When you focus more on anatomy than physiology, you often overpromise and underdeliver. The physiology of our brand also goes back to our company's culture, whether it is billing our teams, client base, partnerships, or overall company's reputation. We must get to that place, where we are delivering that which we are promising. What message are you sending? You may look very good on paper, your flyers may look beautiful, your videos may look beautiful, everything may look professional, you may have a smooth system in place to follow up with your potential customers and clients; however, your personality is unwelcoming. You are nasty to your clients and have a sense of entitlement. People can sense when they are being sold. Build solid relationships. Relationships are the backbone of sales; if they like you, they will follow you and buy from you.

Perfectionist mindset is based on the need to be perfect. We spend most of our time wanting everything to be perfect before we launch the business; we want to make sure that our social media accounts, website, connections, brand identity, etc., are well put together before we ever launch our business. We will even spend years planning a business that we'll never launch. Every single time we look at our business plan, it looks like we're not ready to launch, and that's because we are stuck on being perfect. Let yourself off the hook. Make peace with the fact that it will never be perfect. There will always be something to do; there will always be something to learn. The more we learn, the more we grow; it's going to be new all over again. We will never get it all figured out. The best method to use to overcome perfectionism is to set a plan in place. Once we get that plan in place and have a checklist, it will help us stay on target.

"You cannot hit a target you cannot see, and you cannot see a target you do not have". – Zig Ziglar

Checklist is a great thing for the perfectionist in us. When we are launching a product or service, we will revert to our checklist. Once we have hit everything on our checklist, we are moving onto something else. We will not worry about changing anything related to that project, once we have checked that off our list. We will launch that project and move on.

Chapter 2 - The Sabotaging Mindset

The sabotaging mindset is the mindset that shows up once our business is launched. This mindset is the mindset that tells us that we're not good enough, we can't do it, quit and throw in the towel. It may come through the voice of someone close to us, for example, family members, friends, etc. Sometimes it could even be our own thoughts. Where there is growth, discouragement will always show up. We will often hear, "I know someone that started a business and it didn't work." "What makes you so special?" "Who do you think you are?" These often turn into rejection, and once rejection sets in, it is very difficult to bounce back from it.

Entrepreneurs must keep themselves plugged into things that will keep their passion burning, such as podcast, videos, strategic alliances, magazines, books, networking events, and mentorship programs. During this stage, you will be relying heavily on your support system. Entrepreneurs often sabotage themselves by destroying valuable relationships. It is important to build strong relationships along our entrepreneurial journey. Relationships are necessary to expand and dominate our market-place.

We often get in our own way when we are growing. It is important to remain humble, silence your ego. Arrogance will hurt your business. You are never too big to show your clients and team members respect and appreciation. The thing that is often overlooked in a broken system, is looking at the leadership. If the leadership is broken, that will trickle into the overall success of the business. To overcome this mindset, keep in mind that you are not the only one out there doing what you are doing. There is another business just like yours down the street. Why do I need to purchase your services or work for you if you are going to abuse me?

A great company should not have a high turnover rate. It is important to invest in the right talent. Our team is a vital part of our brand anatomy and physiology. Our clients are expecting to see them when they come there. Business owners often get caught up in replacing people to make their brand stronger. Replacing people weakens our brand, especially for small businesses. We must invest in training and coaching programs for our team. The first impression that someone gets is, they always have new people. What is going on with this company? This company is a joke and they can't keep any employees. They also believe that with all the changes they are not getting the quality services that they deserve.

Imagine going to a doctor's office, and every time you go to that office, you meet a new team of doctors and medical assistants. How would you feel? Surely, you would be questioning the owner's integrity. Think of a few popular Fortune 500 companies that you've been seeing their brand for years. They always have the same people as the face of the brand. Why do you think that is? They understand that those people are a part of their brand identity. Consistency is the solution to the sabotaging mindset. Be consistent with brand anatomy & physiology, and your company will grow. With growth, you must learn the art of letting go.

Chapter 3 - The Fear-Of-Letting-Go Mindset

The fear-of-letting-go mindset is the mindset that keeps us from getting to the next level of our business. This mindset is the mindset that makes people single-handedly break down their business from the inside out. They are afraid that nobody will be able to do it like them. That they are the only one that can run that business. If your business cannot survive a month or two without you, you do not have a business. You have a job, or an expensive full-time hobby. It's like having a new born child, you want the best for your child, and you do not trust anyone with that child. Especially with all the horrible things that we have heard about. Now, it's time to send that child to daycare, and fear starts to set in. We are so attached to our child that we don't want to let them go.

In business, it is the same thing. A lot of entrepreneurs start off as solo entrepreneurs. They are the only one in that business and they play every position. However, when it's time to sit down and give it to the experts, they get insecure. You must be able to give that position over to someone that is skilled in that department that can take the business to the next level. While you trust, you should always verify that the business is running smooth and efficient. You should never be a hands-off owner. It will never work. That is the recipe for disaster and losing the business altogether.

Solo entrepreneurs learn enough to run the business. There are a lot of things that come with running a business and we need to know when to let go. We can only be in one place at a time. Building a strong team is vital to the overall success and growth of the business. It doesn't always take money to build a team; technology allows us to expand our business for little to no cost. We can automate our business as well as B2B collaboration, where we work together with other business owners, that is building a team. We have a team and we do not have to come out of our pockets to pay that business directly. We must let go off the industrial way of doing things and embrace technology, growth, and change. We can contract freelancers to build our teams. We pay them once the work is completed. There are plenty of ways to build a team and expand your business. Do research and find the methods that work best for you. Business is not one-size-fits-all.

Build a business that you are proud to be a part of. How many people have a job, but are not confident enough to tell people the nature of their job? If you dislike your business, no one else will like your business. If you don't like yourself, why would we like you? Do not let insecurity stop you from turning task over to the experts. If the boss is insecure, they will hold their teams back, because they believe that they must be the smartest person in the room. We manage personalities, not people. As bosses, our role is to manage a lot of personalities at one time. We must keep those personalities from erupting on each other. We must empower our teammates to be the best version of themselves as possible. Let people shine. What is a diamond that is hidden?

"A diamond is worthless until you dig it up." - Shanie Salmon-Godfrey

You must put systems in place to allow your business to grow and trust those systems. You must let go in order to elevate.

"Elevation is the result of transformation." – Shanie Salmon-Godfrey

Elevation is on the other side of change. With change comes expansion, but don't get caught up in the busybody mindset.

Chapter 4 - The Busybody Mindset

The busybody mindset can be very catastrophic for any entrepreneur, regardless of how long they have been in business. This mindset will have the entrepreneur, going, going, and going. This mindset is dangerous because entrepreneurs seem to think that they are being productive. It is important to know that you are the secret sauce. The one thing that your competitor doesn't have and will never have is you. You make your brand unique.

Entrepreneurs with this mindset tend to take on a lot more than they can handle; partner up with a lot of people that they should not partner up with; start a lot of business ventures that should've never been started. The one thing that we must remember is, we are our greatest asset. We cannot stretch ourselves too thin. We must take time for our health. Our health is our greatest asset. What is the value of building a business that you are too sick to enjoy? We need to transform our mindset from the need to be busy, to the need for productivity. Our goal is to be more productive and less busy. Busy is not the new productive. For your business to grow, you need to settle down in your business. All your focus needs to be on your business. Once you can step away from your business for a few months and your business continues to grow, then you can take on more ventures.

You cannot say yes to everything. Take the time to write down a one-paragraph message that pleasantly declines new business ventures. Have this ready, because when your business is growing, there will always be people that think that you are a great fit for their business venture. Those ventures will not always align with your mission. Keep your blinders on, align with businesses that compliments what you are already doing.

Sometimes we will be caught off-guard. When we are caught off-guard, we find ourselves in situations that we are trying to get out of. You do not have time to be distracted. Have your note ready. While you are being pitched this new business venture, you are reading your message so you know exactly what your response should be. In the first 3 years of your business, you should not be launching any new ventures. Most businesses fail in the first 2-3 years, because entrepreneurs do not make enough money to stay in business. If you are transitioning from an employee to a full-time entrepreneur, in the first 3 years of your business, stay in your job. It will develop skills and leadership abilities that will propel you into success.

You will learn from the failures and successes of your employer. The first 3 years is crucial to your business. You must master productivity and consistency. You must remain 100 percent focused on your business. This is the stage that we learn how to serve our customers and our team members.

Chapter 5 - The Servant Mindset

The servant mindset is the mindset that we all need to master. Once we understand servitude, our business will go to the next level, thrive, and have the potential to earn unlimited income. The servant mindset is the mindset that allows us to solve problems and provide solutions. The purpose of every business is to solve a problem. What problem are you solving? Who are you serving? Keep in mind that you cannot help everybody. Some people will not like you, no matter what you do. You cannot please everyone, that's okay. Don't worry about the people that don't like you and focus on the ones that do like you. The anatomy & physiology of your brand will attract the people that want to do business with your company. Your goal is serving those people when they come to you.

Share your story. Your story is your testimony; people are more interested in how you have lived through their pain and not so much how much you know. Show me how you have lived through my pain. We are in an overly self-medicated society, no one wants to feel pain. In order to be a good servant, you need to be able to relate to the pain of your customers. Don't make assumptions that there are a lot of tools and resources that you can use to get their feedback on what's causing them pain. Be accountable to your customers and be an active listener. You cannot serve your audience if you do not listen to learn from them. There is always something to learn in successes and failures. Keep your ears open and boss up.

Boss Up

B-Build

O-Organize

S-Sustain

S-Spread

Now that you have mastered the 5 entrepreneurial mindsets, it's time to B.O.S.S Up. Build with passion. Focus on culture.

Build

To build, you must diminish insecurities. Focus on the art of people sculpting. Leaders are not produced overnight. They take years of sculpting and cultivating. Focus on the person behind the skills. Put a value on the person and not the skillset. There is an old saying that, "You catch more bees with honey, than vinegar." You can get a lot more out of people if they truly believe that you want the best for them. That you genuinely want to see them become the best version of themselves. That means inside and outside of your organization. Make your mission clear throughout your branding message and organization structure; remember that they will follow the footprints of the leader. A great leader will provoke growth; people will grow by being around that leader.

Organize

The bigger they are, the harder they fall. Empires crumble for lack of organization. Organization doesn't always mean how neat and tidy your workstations are. It doesn't matter how well your calendar is well put together, that you are always on time, true organization comes from how well departmental structures are organized. Are you working out of a silo or a cohesive unit? I read a study that said, "The goal of every company should be to have less meetings." Silos generate meetings that don't accomplish anything. They are unproductive, with frequent meetings, and lack consistency. A team that is divided cannot stand. Lack of organization drives high turnover rate, which will leak money out of your pocket, and eventually shut your business down. Lead without walls. Every position is important, no matter how big or small the titles may be. Break the walls down and keep it together. People will develop skills that will push them to want more, don't hold them back.

Sustain

To sustain your brand, your company must be transparent. Lack of transparency will lead to distrust. Be transparent with your team, no matter what. The water cooler talks are not good for any business, especially in the digital age. The water cooler talks are now virtual water coolers that can spread like a volcano when those talks erupt. It is important to address them, and do so honestly. If your team must find out about changes in your business from the customers, you won't have a business for too long.

In addition to being transparent, you need to take care of yourself in the process. Self-care is important to keep you from imploding. Take time to rest and develop new skills. Being a business owner is being a professional student, there is always something new to learn. When you learn, you grow. Don't keep the growth to yourself. Spread it amongst your team. Spreading knowledge will help you dominate your marketplace. Remember, the team member might be more knowledgeable about a subject that you are not skilled on, but in the end, it is helping your company to grow. Don't make them feel inferior.

Spread

Spread your passion like a wild fire. Show us what you are working with. Hire people by getting them fired up about your brand. The passion is the driving force of the success of your business. Your hard work will not go to waste. This is where the sculpting and cultivating come into play. All the hard work that you put into your team will now start to generate a ROI. A return on your investment. This return on your investment is going to take your businesses to territories that you didn't think were possible. There is power in numbers. You can reach more people in different parts of the world by letting your team duplicate and replicate the systems that you put in place.

Summary

It all starts with the mind. Before we even put that business plan down on paper, we formulate it in our minds. We will become a lot of different people to reach our promised land. We must fight through the 5 entrepreneurial mindset and then boss up. Once we get rid of the need to always be right and understand that business is not perfect and will never go the way that we planned on it going, we're one step closer to success. We must stop the sabotage. Stop talking ourselves out of growth. Automate that business and let go and let's grow. Be productive, not busy. Productivity is going to keep your brand consistent and allow you to better serve your marketplace. To serve your marketplace, you must solve problems.

Entrepreneurship is not easy. It takes years to develop the necessary skills that we need to run an effective business, build brand loyalty, and make a steady flow of income. Do not rush the process. Do not worry about failing, everybody fails. Learn the lesson attached to that failure, stop the negative self-talk, and boss up.

"What's a diamond without the shine?"-Shanie Salmon-Godfrey

BIO
About the Author

Shanie Salmon-Godfrey, NCMA, MAA

Shanie Salmon-Godfrey is a mighty, powerful, consecrated woman of God who is a visionary. Shanie Salmon-Godfrey is a proven visionary. This woman of God is married and has one son. She is a strategic leadership coach, media brand coach, transformational speaker, and serial entrepreneur. Her mission is to empower humanity to build a legacy that lasts by using their gifts and talents to Transform, Elevate, and Empower.

Shanie Salmon-Godfrey has birthed: Legacy Consulting Firm, Elevation TV Network, Elevation Radio Network, and Gifted Magazine. She is the host of Break-Fast W/ Shanie Show and The Gifted Show. In addition, her podcast, Let's Talk T.E.E, is available on iTunes and Spotify.

Shanie Salmon-Godfrey is also the author of: The Entrepreneurial Mindset and Face The Lion, which is currently being penned.

A Message from Shanie

Build the future of your business today. Everything you pour into your business today, will determine the strength of your business tomorrow.

Don't Build a company, Build a Legacy.

"The Greatest Businesses are the ones that are built with passion."

– Shanie Salmon-Godfrey

www.shaniesalmon.com

www.ingramcontent.com/pod-product-compliance
Lightning Source LLC
Chambersburg PA
CBHW030738180526
45157CB00008BA/3231